T0011381

WHAT YOU NEVER KNEW ABOUT

ARIANA
GRANDE

by Mari Schuh

CAPSTONE PRESS
a capstone imprint

For Aleyna

This is an unauthorized biography.

Published by Spark, an imprint of Capstone
1710 Roe Crest Drive, North Mankato, Minnesota 56003
capstonepub.com

Library of Congress Cataloging-in-Publication Data
Names: Schuh, Mari C., 1975– author.
Title: What you never knew about Ariana Grande / by Mari Schuh.
Description: North Mankato, Minnesota : Spark, an imprint of Capstone, 2023. | Series: Behind the scenes biographies | Includes bibliographical references and index. | Audience: Ages 9–11 | Audience: Grades 4–6 |Summary: "What are the names of Ariana Grande's pets? Who was her first celebrity crush? Go behind the scenes to discover little-known facts about this superstar singer and actor. High-interest details and bold photos of her fascinating life will enthrall readers"— Provided by publisher.
Identifiers: LCCN 2022022087 (print) | LCCN 2022022088 (ebook) | ISBN 9781669002857 (hardcover) | ISBN 9781669040514 (paperback) | ISBN 9781669002819 (pdf) | ISBN 9781669002833 (kindle edition)
Subjects: LCSH: Grande, Ariana—Juvenile literature. | Singers—United States—Biography—Juvenile literature.
Classification: LCC ML3930.G724 S35 2023 (print) | LCC ML3930.G724 (ebook) | DDC 782.42164092 [B]—dc23/eng/20220506
LC record available at https://lccn.loc.gov/2022022087
LC ebook record available at https://lccn.loc.gov/2022022088

Editorial Credits
Editor: Erika L. Shores; Designer: Heidi Thompson; Media Researcher: Jo Miller; Production Specialist: Tori Abraham

◇ ◇ ◇ ◇ ◇ ◇ ◇ ◇ ◇ ◇ ◇ ◇ ◇ ◇ ◇ ◇ ◇ ◇ ◇ ◇

POP SUPERSTAR

TABLE OF CONTENTS

Words in **bold** are in the glossary.

Fans all over the world love Ariana Grande. She's a pop superstar. Think you are the biggest **Arianator** around? Did you know that some of her family used to say their last name in a different way? It sounded like "Gran-dee."

What else might surprise you about Ariana? Let's find out!

ARIANA'S
NUMBER ONES

Are you a super fan? How many of Ariana's favorites do you know?

1. Favorite holiday?

2. Favorite artist?

3. Favorite fruit?

4. Favorite meat?

5. Bonus points for young Ariana's favorite celebrity! He was her first celebrity crush!

1. Halloween 2. Imogen Heap 3. Strawberries

4. None! Ariana is vegan. 5. Jim Carrey

Ari played Cat Valentine on the TV shows *Victorious* and *Sam & Cat*. She loves to wear cat eye makeup and cat ears. So, are cats her favorite pet? No. Ari is allergic to cats. She can't get enough of her pups. She has plenty of pooches—12 **rescue dogs**!

Love is everything when it comes to Ari and her pets. She loves to give them fun names. Two of her dogs are named Snape and Lily. They are characters from Harry Potter.

Ari also has a pet pig named Piggy Smallz. Wait. What? Yep, a pet pig. It is named after rapper Biggie Smalls.

ARIANA BY THE NUMBERS

Elizabeth Gillies, Mark Indelicato, Ariana Grande, and Miranda Cosgrove backstage at the musical *13*

Ariana was born June 26, 1993. At age 15, she got a role in the Broadway musical titled *13*. Ari made her *Thank U, Next* album in just two weeks. It came out in 2019. It sold more than 360,000 copies in its first week.

FACT

In 2002, Ari sang the national anthem at a Florida Panthers hockey game. She was 8 years old.

Imagine having Ari's big numbers. Photos of her getting married got more than 25 million likes on Instagram. Her songs have been **streamed** more than 23 billion times. That's billion with a letter *b*. As in a BIG deal.

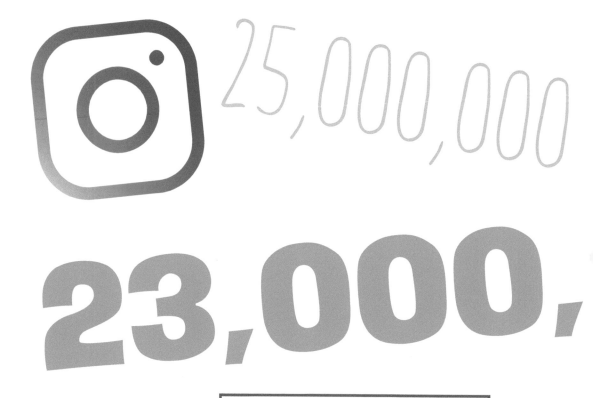

FACT

Ari never had formal voice training. She learned to read sheet music when she played the French horn.

000,000

STRIKE
A POSE

Ari is a **fashionista**. She often pairs short skirts or big sweatshirts with thigh-high boots. She wears fancy high heels. She also wears long gloves, neck scarves, and leather pants.

Ari's style is fun and fancy. She was pretty in pink at an awards show in 2018. One gorgeous gown was inspired by the ceiling of the famous Sistine Chapel. Ari looked like a walking piece of art!

Ari is famous for her ponytail. It's sleek and sky-high. She's been rocking it since she was a kid. Now her pony is super long. But it's actually hair **extensions**. By the way, her real hair is curly!

OUT OF THIS
WORLD

Ari loves **sci-fi**. So it's no surprise that her glam makeup line has a space-age feel.

Ari's makeup line is called r.e.m. beauty. She has a song called "R.E.M." OMG! The letters R, E, sound like Ari.

"You can never have enough makeup, just like you can never have enough music."

—Ariana Grande (*Allure*, October 2021)

FACT
Ari is a Harry Potter fan. She named one of her eyeshadows Plumbledore. It is named after Professor Dumbledore.

HEAD IN THE
CLOUDS

Arianators know that Ari loves clouds. In 2020, Ari dressed up as a cloud at the **Grammys**. She has a cloud perfume and a cloud tattoo. She even had a cloud coffee drink at Starbucks. Her favorite emoji? The cloud, of course!

TOTALLY
FLIPPED

What's up with Ari's upside-down photos, videos, words, and tattoos? At her wedding in 2021, she wore one earring upside down. It's cool for sure. But there's more to it. Ari says it means she is grateful for the lowest, or upside-down, times in her life.

FACT
Ari is amazing at celebrity impressions. She can sound just like Rihanna, Shakira, and Britney Spears.

A **DREAMY** ROLE

Kristin Chenoweth played the original Glinda in the Broadway play *Wicked*.

Ari will play Glinda the Good Witch in the movie *Wicked*. Ari saw the play *Wicked* way back in 2011. She **tweeted** how much she wanted to play Glinda someday. The role is a dream come true!

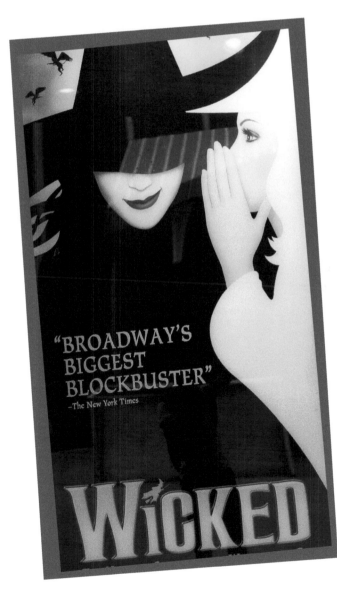

Glossary

Arianator (ari-uh-NAY-tur)—what an Ariana Grande fan is called

extensions (ek-STEN-shuns)—fake or real hair that is attached to your own hair to add length or volume

fashionista (FASH-uhn-ees-ta)—someone who works in or has strong knowledge of fashion

Grammys (GRAM-eez)—an award show for achievement in the music industry

rescue dogs (RESS-kyoo DAWGS)—dogs that had been homeless

sci-fi (SYE-FI)—short for science fiction; science-fiction stories tell about the way real or pretend science can change people and the world

stream (STREEM)—to get music and videos on a cellphone, computer, or other electronic device without having to download it from the internet

tweet (TWEET)—to make a post on Twitter, an online message service

Read More

Bach, Greg. *Ariana Grande*. Hollywood, FL: Mason Crest, 2022.

London, Martha. *Ariana Grande.* Lake Elmo, MN: Focus Readers, 2021.

Schwartz, Heather E. *Ariana Grande: Music Superstar*. Minneapolis: Lerner Publications, 2021.

Internet Sites

50 Facts About Ariana Grande
thefactsite.com/ariana-grande-facts/

All of Ariana Grande's Scene-Stealing Outfits on 'The Voice' so far
insider.com/ariana-grande-fashion-the-voice-outfits-photos-2021-10

Ariana Grande Official Website
arianagrande.com

Index

About the Author

Mari Schuh's love of reading began with cereal boxes at the kitchen table. Today she is the author of hundreds of nonfiction books for young readers. Mari lives in the Midwest with her husband and their sassy house rabbit. Learn more about her at marischuh.com.